I0165217

THE FAITH PROCESS

BY

Minister DeWanda Gill

Horton International Ministries, Inc., Haines City, FL

Published in Winter Haven, FL. Published by
Horton International Ministries.
All inquiries should be addressed to:
hortoninternationalministries@gmail.com
This and other Horton International Ministries
books may be purchased in bulk for educational,
business, motivational coaching, fundraising, or sales
promotions. For more information email:
hortoninternationalministries@gmail.com
Scripture references noted. Print 1, April, 2020
ISBN #: 978-0-578-68328-7

Dedication

This book is dedicated to my beloved, deceased husband of 37 years, Frank A. Gill, who passed January 23, 2020. Also, I dedicate this book to my three precious children: Chavis (Camielle), D'Andra, and Aaron. You all were there to witness many tears and many misunderstandings of the way our Heavenly Father moves.

I am also dedicating this book to the many people who have been born again; JESUS is your SAVIOR, and, you truly believe in our FATHER above. YET there is something missing. You have FAITH but nothing seems to be manifesting. Well, let me help you out, I am going to share some things with you which will turn your pain into gain. Be encouraged and go through the process. GOD is preparing something BIG for you, but you must go through The Process.

Horton International Ministries, Inc., Haines City, FL

Hebrews 11:1 (NKJV) - Now faith is the substance of things hoped for, the evidence of things not seen.

Hebrews 11:6 (NKJV) - But without faith it is impossible to please HIM, for he who comes to GOD must believe that HE is, and that HE is a rewarder of those who diligently seek HIM.

Minister DeWanda Gill

Table of Contents

Horton International Ministries, Inc., Haines City, FL

Chapter 1

The Process Begins

My FATHER, I can remember when I first started this walk. Oh my GOD how beautiful everything seemed. Little did I know The Faith Process would carry me through many different stages of life. Some stages would be so easy, and then there were those tests that would feel like I was literally dying!!!!!!

Yes, you heard me, TESTS!!!!!!

I wish someone would have told me about the development that comes with being a Christian. Just as our Savior had a cross to bear, in The Faith Process you will have many crosses to bear; but of course, nothing could ever compare to the price JESUS paid at the cross.

If someone had warned me in advance I would have known how to or how not to react. I would have known my tears do not move GOD; only my faith does. Why didn't the preacher warn me about the days that I would desire to grow wings and fly away or step into the path of a moving bus? Why didn't they tell me most of the battle was in my mind? Nevertheless I will share some things that were not said or I had taken for granted.

In The Faith Process we can take nothing for granted because we are dealing with principalities, fighting "... *against powers, against the rulers of the darkness of this age, against spiritual host of wickedness in*

the HEAVENLY Places" Ephesians 6:12 (NKJV).
This stuff is REAL and they play for KEEPS!
Fighting this force is part of The Faith Process.
GREATER is HE that is in me than any evil force in
this world.

When we come to CHRIST we come as
children in school; the first couple of years are
victory, victory, victory with little effort on our part.

I can remember coming to CHRIST and
making a vow to always pay my tithe. Over the last
31 years we have been consistent 90% of the time. I
knew the tithe and offering the first couple of years
was to see our FATHER rebuke the devourer; it was
such a joy.

YES, the word was alive and it was working for us. Little did I know I was a child in grade school. One of my gifts is a giver, so coming to CHRIST and paying tithe and offering was a small thing to me. I did it without sweat. Yes, doors were opened, and increase came so freely.

It came so freely!

Keep in mind we were still in grade school; we were babies. The more we gave, the more we received. We can't beat our FATHER giving no matter how hard we try. We belonged to Turner's Faith Temple, Bridgeport, CT. We were not taught much about giving; however, we just knew it was the right thing to do. We gave and our FATHER blessed us with three beautiful and brilliant children: Chavis, D'Andra and Aaron, who were taught to give.

Many times we would give and it would come right back. When I was nine months pregnant with Aaron and needed at least $500 to purchase some of the things I would need for an infant, it was tough. At this point in our lives we were living from paycheck to paycheck.

We continued to do what was right and that was giving our FATHER what was HIS and trusting HIM for everything we needed for the baby. A few sisters from the church got together and gave me a beautiful shower and I received almost everything I needed. PRAISE our GOD!!!

GOD takes care of HIS own!

Enter now into middle school of The Faith Process.

Chapter 2

Trust GOD

Horton International Ministries, Inc., Haines City, FL

One of the many Bridgeport Hospital Emergency Room trips with Aaron, I remember his throat had begun to close from an allergic reaction to nuts. Doctors and nurses were everywhere. The doctor said he needed to put a trachea into Aaron's throat.

I started to pray and to believe GOD to turn the situation around. The doctor said "if this child dies you will be held responsible." I STOOD my ground, believing my GOD because nothing is too hard for our GOD!

Nothing is Too Hard for God!

The nurse came in and said, "I don't know what you are doing but continue to do it." I knew my FATHER would take care of him and, of course, HE did.

I am still in middle school watching our FATHER teach us The Faith Process. Our FATHER is so FAITHFUL in protecting and providing for us. He keeps us from danger seen and unseen.

My son, Aaron, was called a prophet from my womb, so coming up there were many attempts to take his life and also my life at an early age. There were at least six attempts on each of our lives, but my FATHER is so FAITHFUL.

One particular time we were invited to a friend's house for a pool party. I can remember being in four feet of water with Aaron in my arms and it seemed the place where I was standing became six feet. I can't swim with my child in my arms, I am going down. I hear my friend ask, "Can you swim?"

I said to her, "get my son" and I threw him to her. I was going down and in my physical mind I was convinced I would drown.

But, when purpose is on your life you can't die! I honestly don't know what happened, but I ended up on the side of the pool as my friend looked at me and asked, "How did you get here?"

At this point I was looking dumb-founded knowing there was an angel looking over us. My GOD and my FATHER saved both of us.

You Can't Die!

FATHER you are so AMAZING! When we first accepted JESUS as LORD and SAVIOR the battles seemed like a piece of cake. It took me a few years to realize our walk with GOD is just like being in grade school. We are graded as we go from one grade level to another in The Faith Process and we are tested on every level.

Sometimes during the testing the teacher will be quiet. Sometimes we will feel like we have been forgotten. But, HE is there because HE said HE would never leave us or forsake us.

During these times in our life we must learn to first deal with our mind. So many different negative thoughts bombard our minds. We, as children of the Most High GOD, must cast down imaginations and every high thing that exalts itself against the knowledge of GOD and bring into captivity every thought to the obedience of CHRIST.

In other words, when you start thinking on negative things use the authority our FATHER has given you through The Blood of JESUS CHRIST and the power of the WORD. Think on the WORD of GOD because the WORD is ALIVE.

Our FATHER spoke that to me many years ago, but it took me some years to learn how to war with the enemy with the WORD of GOD. The WORD of GOD is ALIVE and POWERFUL! The Word is sharper than the sharpest two –edged sword, cutting between soul and spirit, joints and marrow; it judges the attitudes of the heart. The Word of The LORD is proven; HE is a shield to all who trust in HIM.

We must become fearless Christians to see the supernatural in our life. We must have confidence in the WORD of GOD! We must not look at our problems, but hold onto GOD'S Word. HIS promises are so POWERFUL!

GOD told Ezekiel to prophesy to a valley full of dry bones. So, he spoke with BOLDNESS, life to the dry bones, and they became an exceedingly great army. We must speak life in our dead situations.

In the Word of GOD we find hope; in my affliction I will hope in the Word of GOD. We have hope in the Word of GOD. We have AUTHORITY in the Word of GOD. As we speak the Word, watch it work in our lives. The Word is our life line.

Chapter 3

Only Trust God

In my first few years of salvation and walking with GOD it was easy to trust GOD. While in grade school the tests are easy. There have been many tests and trials and mess ups on my part. Many times, I have felt forgotten, depressed, suicidal, discouraged, and worthless. Yet, our faith has a PROCESS and a place of development.

Without complete trust in our FATHER we will not win over the adversary. Salvation will lead you into many faith fights. We must continue to trust GOD.

Trust is to believe that someone or something is reliable, good, honest, effective, and also exudes confidence or reliance. GOD waits to see if we really trust HIM. We need confidence for every day. Saying we trust HIM is so much easier than standing after having done all to stand.

We must not cast away our confidence which hath great recompense of reward. We must refuse to throw away our confidence no matter what we see.

We must trust GOD in the hard places in our wilderness. Trust our FATHER with all your heart. We must trust even though we cannot see HIM or feel HIM. Many times I have felt like throwing in the towel, because the cares of the world just seem to be too much. I knew I could not give up or give in, because our FATHER is able to do all things. So, total trust is so important.

Total Trust in God!

We must learn to trust even in the pain. Even though we don't know when the pain will end, we must still trust GOD. Many times GOD will carry you through hard and difficult times. He will give you a promise and bring you through a drought! It is all a part of The Faith Process. We must take authority over the devil in the name of JESUS, we must trust the Faith Process.

Stand firm on the Word of GOD and know that authority has been given in the spiritual and natural realm. We must trust GOD in turmoil. We must get to the place of rest. Trust commands rest, and rest commands manifestation.

We must trust what GOD said and not be troubled. **Our FATHER is not a man that HE should lie. Neither the Son of man that HE should repent.** Trust GOD through it all. Has HE said, and will HE not do it, or has HE spoken and will HE not fulfill it?

We trust GOD by believing HIS WORD is alive and true and it is working in our life. The enemy will do all he can to bring confusion in our lives. His goal is to slow down the process of our spiritual development. The enemy puts up smoke-screens which make our lives seem to be a contradiction of the Word of GOD. We must learn to stay focused on the Word of GOD. Decree and declare the Word and know it is working for you.

The same power that raised JESUS from the dead dwells within us. That is a lot of POWER & AUTHORITY. We must find courage in the Word of GOD. In the time of courage we must not fear. We will not fear, but we will TRUST our FATHER with our whole heart.

My life has been full of pain many, many times. The enemy has tried many tactics to make me throw in the towel, but I had to hold on to my confidence and labor to get to the place of rest. That place of knowing our FATHER will make a difference.

HE is the difference!

Many times it seems our circumstances go from bad to worst. We must remember GOD is the difference. Many times it seemed our FATHER was so far from us! I would say FATHER you said you were close to the broken hearted. HE would remind me weeping may endure for a night, but joy cometh in the morning. Sometimes the fog sets in, but we must stand on the promises of GOD". "FATHER I know you are in control". We must stand firm and know HE will never fail us. Trust GOD and know HE is going to do what HE said HE would. We must go through the FAITH PROCESS!

Chapter 4

The Process

The Faith Process is when GOD brings us into a place where difficulties are, where pressure mounts, where everything is so difficult that we know there are no possibilities on the human side. GOD must do it. All these places are in GOD'S plan. We are in the process where GOD allows trials, difficulties, temptations, and perplexities to come along our path. This is making and molding you into our FATHER'S image.

This process, at times, will have you feeling abandoned and at times you will literally feel like you are dying, but you will not. Our FATHER is ridding you of all things not like HIM. This process will many times cause you to feel like you are losing your mind.

It is in the Faith Process where you are being prepared for greatness. GOD is with you in the Process; HE is molding you into greatness. You will not feel great, but it is working together for your good. It may not feel good, but you are building SPIRITUAL MUSCLE!

Pearls are beautiful gems our FATHER has blessed us with, but pearls are made from irritations. Our test is to bring out the best in us. While in the Process we should ask ourselves these questions. Have I grown? Do I really trust GOD? Do I see myself as GOD does?

We must always find the treasure in our trials and know that the Process builds our character and humbles us. In other words, it's less of self and more of GOD in our lives. When we are in the valley of Process, we learn the most about GOD. In the valley of Process the purifying of pain is at work in you. GOD has a purpose for our pain. GOD is up to something in our experience.

The right way for you to respond is:

✓ Surrender to God.

✓ Believe God will use you for His good.

✓ Rest in His wisdom, His love, and His power.

✓ Give God thanks.

The Process will make us more useful to GOD. HE knows what it will take to make you. So be not weary in well doing, because every time you past a test you are headed for a promotion.

There is a PEARL in YOU! GOD loves you too much to leave you alone. We say stop to uncomfortable situations-GOD says "Not yet"! He sees you as a finished product, PURE GOLD or that precious PEARL that is birthed from irritations.

Our FATHER will allow the cares of the world to come in to test our character and to show us what we are really made of. During this time we are probably dealing with the contradictions of life, yet we must trust the process HE has allowed to come our way.

We must call those things that are not as though they are. We will see the manifestation as we believe GOD. Many times you may feel forgotten or forsaken but this is what our FATHER says, "When you pass through the waters, I will be with you; and when you pass through the rivers, they will not sweep over you. When you walk through the fire, you will not be burned; the flames will not set you ablaze". Isaiah 43:2 (NIV)

Trust the Process!

Trust The Process. GOD has us; GOD with us is more than the whole world against us. Trust The Faith Process and don't rely on your own understanding.

We must see the GOD given picture and plant the seed by staying focused and go through The Process. Just in case you didn't know, FAITH is now and now is a PROCESS of EXPECTATION and finally MANIFESTATION. The Process will bring out all kinds of emotions, which is geared to make us more like CHRIST.

The Process shows you, you and your many flaws! When we are being molded and tested, if we allow The Process to work, we will become more like GOD. Our character is truly revealed when pressure is applied. The Process is when GOD brings us into a place where the difficulties are, where the pressure is, where the hard corner is, and where everything is so difficult that you know there are no possibilities on the human side. GOD must do it. All these places are part of The Process, and they are in GOD'S plan.

The Process is to reveal our strengths and weaknesses; our goal should always be to follow through The Process and not avoid it! We must stand firm in the midst of The Process. Trust GOD to make it all right. Trust HIM in your darkest hours.

Minister DeWanda Gill

There will be times in your life when it will feel like even GOD has left you, but rest assured you are not alone. Stand on HIS Word, speak HIS Word, and mediate on HIS Word. Our GOD is able to do exceeding above what we can ask or think. We must stand on the Word and know HIS Word is ALIVE!

Chapter 5

Winning

The greatest battle to win will be control of your mind. Your adversary will bring many negative thoughts to your mind. Refuse to entertain them. Pull down every negative thought from the onset. See the end from the beginning, as GOD does.

The Process is making us more like GOD. Don't dwell on the negative images; use your imagination to see the end, the graduation. Your darkest hours are the hardest when it seems it is all falling apart. We must remember that the stumbling blocks in our life are designed to make us strong and move us into another dimension of power. Don't allow them to trip you up.

We must daily brain-dump all negative thoughts. Negative thoughts must be dealt with for us to emerge into our destiny. We must think about what we are thinking about. Guarding our mind is the most important part of The Process. I said earlier, but this is worth REPEATING! We must pull down every imagination that exalts itself against the knowledge of GOD and bring into captivity every thought to the obedience of CHRIST. This is so important in The Faith Process. We must see it the way God does!

See it the way God Does!

The real battle ground is never your situation; it is the battle of the mind. Your perception cannot be as the natural realm, regardless of how bleak it looks. Your struggles are an indication that breakthrough is on the horizon for you.

Refuse to allow the enemy to dump his negative thoughts in your mind. To win in The Faith Process we must pray and believe GOD. We must cancel every naysayer including the one in our minds, and rest in our confidence in GOD.

No time to fear, no time to panic, trusting only in the true and living GOD! Trust God and renew your mind to the promises of GOD in The Faith Process. As we win the battle over our mind and rest in our God, we shall see the manifestation of HIS promises

Be encouraged. GOD has not forgotten you. HE is making you more like HIM. HE is refining you not as silver, but gold. HE is testing you in the furnace of affliction which I choose to call The Faith Process. BE ENCOURAGED and know GREATNESSS shall be your REWARD!

About the Author

Dewanda Gill is no stranger to faith. She is known for three major gifts; her faith, her giving, and, her hunger for the Spirit of God. Over 36 years of dedication to God, Dewanda has been widely used by the Spirit of God. She moves strongly in these gifts of the Spirit. She flows in the gifts of Knowledge and Wisdom. She has been used greatly in the Power of Intercession. DeWanda's hunger for the Word of God brings her before many to encourage and confirm that which the Lord has spoken.

As a powerful Intercessor, she has witnessed the hand of God bring deliverance to the masses on various topics that she has prayed. She has prayed people through many personal battles.

DeWanda is a Woman of God that is driven by a heart of generosity. She has been a great aide and support to many leaders of the body of Christ. This Woman of God currently serves under the leadership of Apostle Stanley and Lady Williams, The Church 3:20, Jacksonville, FL.

She longs to see the manifestation of the sons of God that will bring to her Father the greatest harvest that the body of Christ shall witness.

My
Next
Book

"The Healing Process"
Coming soon!

Look for it!

DeWanda Gill

Minister DeWanda Gill

Horton International Ministries, Inc., Haines City, FL